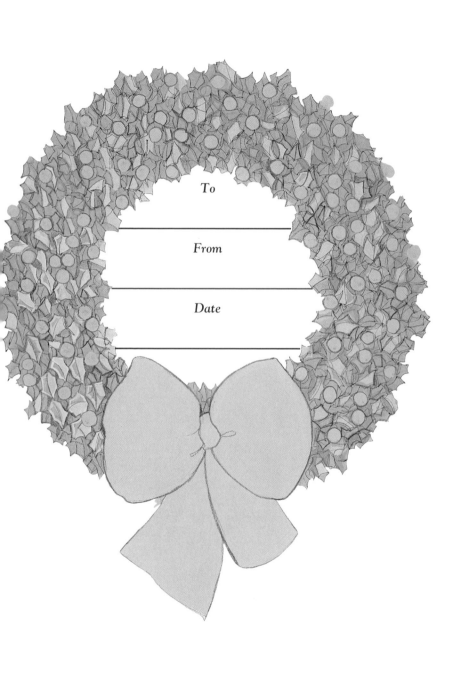

To

_____

From

_____

Date

_____

Christmas Angels

The Helen Steiner Rice Foundation

Whatever the celebration, whatever the day, whatever the event, whatever the occasion, Helen Steiner Rice possessed the ability to express the appropriate feeling for that particular moment in time.

A happening became happier, a sentiment more sentimental, a memory more memorable because of her deep sensitivity to put into understandable language the emotion being experienced. Her positive attitude, her concern for others, and her love of God are identifiable threads woven into her life, her works. . . and even her death.

Prior to her passing, she established the Helen Steiner Rice Foundation, a nonprofit corporation whose purpose is to award grants to worthy charitable programs and aid the elderly, the needy, and the poor. In her lifetime, these were the individuals about whom Mrs. Rice was greatly concerned.

Royalties from the sale of this book will add to the financial capabilities of the Helen Steiner Rice Foundation. Each year this foundation presents grants to various qualified, worthwhile, and charitable programs. Because of her foresight, her caring, and her deep convictions, Helen Steiner Rice continues to touch a countless number of lives. Thank you for your assistance in helping to keep Helen's dream alive.

Virginia J. Ruehlmann, Administrator
The Helen Steiner Rice Foundation
Suite 2100, Atrium Two
221 East Fourth Street
Cincinnati, Ohio 45202

Christmas Angels

Verses by Helen Steiner Rice

Compiled by Virginia J. Ruehlmann

Illustrations by Samuel J. Butcher

Fleming H. Revell
A Division of Baker Book House Co
Grand Rapids, Michigan 49516

The endsheets,
enhanced with real flower petals,
ferns, and other botanicals,
are from
"The Petals Everlasting Collection"
manufactured by Permalin Products.

Text copyright 1994 by Helen Steiner Rice Foundation
Art copyright 1994 by PRECIOUS MOMENTS, Inc.

Scripture quotationsare from the King James Version

Published by Fleming H. Revell,
a division of Baker Book House
P.O. Box 6287, Grand Rapids, Michigan 49516-6287

Printed in the United States of America.

Library of Congress Cataloging-in-Publication Data

Rice, Helen Steiner.
    Precious moments : Christmas angels / verses by Helen Steiner Rice ;
compiled by Virginia J. Ruehlmann ; illustrations by Samuel J. Butcher.
      p.   cm.
    ISBN 0-8007-7140-0
    1. Christian Poetry, American. 2. Christmas – Poetry. 3. Angels –
Poetry. I. Ruehlmann, Virginia J. II. Butcher, Samuel J. (Samuel
John), 1939– ill. III. Title. IV. Title: Christmas Angels.
PS3568.I28P734   1994
811'.54 – dc20   94–17018

Contents

C is for the Christ Child,
a child of love and light.

H is for the heavens
that were bright that holy night.

R is for the radiance
of the star that led the way.

I is for the lowly inn
where the infant Jesus lay.

S is for the shepherds
who behold the Christmas star.

T is for the tidings
that the angels told afar.

M is for the magi
with their gifts of myrrh and gold.

A is for the angels
who were awesome to behold.

S is for the Savior
who was born to save all men.

Together this spells **C**hristmas,
which we celebrate again.

The Annunciation

And in the sixth month
the angel Gabriel was sent from God
unto a city of Galilee, named Nazareth,
To a virgin espoused to a man
whose name was Joseph
and the virgin's name was Mary.
And the angel came in unto her, and said,
"Hail, thou that art highly favoured,
the Lord is with thee:
blessed art thou among women. . .
And behold thou shalt conceive in thy womb,
and bring forth a son,
and shalt call his name
JESUS."

Luke 1:28-31

The Song of Mary

My soul doth magnify the Lord,
And my spirit hath rejoiced in God my Saviour.
For he hath regarded the low estate
of his handmaiden:
for, behold, from henceforth
all generations shall call me blessed.
For he that is mighty
hath done to me great things:
and holy is his name.
And his mercy is on them that fear him
from generation to generation.
He hath put down the mighty from their seats,
and exalted them of low degree.
He hath filled the hungry with good things;
and the rich he hath sent empty away.
He hath helped his servant Israel,
in remembrance of his mercy;
as he spake to our father,
to Abraham,
and to his seed
forever.

Luke 1:46-55

$\mathcal{B}$ehold!
I bring you good tidings,
the angels sang that night–
the night that Jesus Christ was born
to be this dark world's light
And though we were not there
to hear the song the shepherds heard,
We know he lived and died for us,
for we have our Father's word.

The Shepherds and the Angels

And, lo, the angel of the Lord
came upon them (the shepherds)
and the glory of the Lord shone round about them
and they were sore afraid.
And the angel said unto them:
"Fear not: for, behold, I bring you
good tidings of great joy,
which shall be to all people.
For unto you is born this day
in the city of David
a Saviour which is Christ the Lord . . .
And suddenly there was with the angel
a multitude of the heavenly host
praising God, and saying,
"Glory to God in the highest,
and on earth peace,
good will toward men."

Luke 2:9-11; 13-14

13

$\mathcal{G}$lad tidings herald
the Christ Child's birth–
"Joy to the world"
and "Peace on earth,"
"Glory to God". . .
Let all men rejoice
and harken
once more to the angel's voice.

$\mathcal{I}$t matters not who
or what you are–
all men
can behold the Christmas star.
For the star that shone
is shining still
in the hearts of men
of peace and good will.

CLICK

$\mathcal{I}$t offers the answer
to every man's need,
regardless of color
or race
or creed. . .

So, joining together
in brotherly love,
let us worship again
our father above.
Forgetting
our own
little,
selfish
desires,
May we seek
what the star of Christmas inspires.

*C*hristmas is a season
A time for gifts and presents
for giving and for taking.
A festive, friendly, happy time
when everyone will say,
May cheer, good will, and laughter
be yours this Christmas Day.

Joseph and the Angel

*But while he [Joseph] thought on these things,
behold, the angel of the Lord
appeared to him in a dream, saying,
"Joseph, thou son of David,
fear not to take unto thee
Mary thy wife:
for that which is conceived in her
is of the Holy Ghost.
And she shall bring forth a son,
and thou shalt call his name JESUS:
for he shall save his people
from their sins."*

Matthew 1:20-21

*G*od wants us to be happy
on the birthday of his Son.
And that is why this season
is such a joyous one...

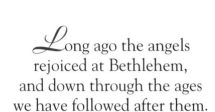

$\mathcal{L}$ong ago the angels
rejoiced at Bethlehem,
and down through the ages
we have followed after them.

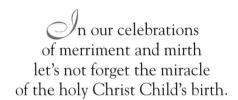

In our celebrations
of merriment and mirth
let's not forget the miracle
of the holy Christ Child's birth.

$\mathcal{B}$y keeping Christ in Christmas
we are helping to fulfill
the glad tidings of the angels–
peace on earth, to men: good will.

$\mathcal{G}$lory to God in the highest
and peace on earth to men. . .

$\mathscr{M}$ay the Christmas song
the angels sang
stir in our hearts again.

*A*nd bring a new awareness
that the fate of every nation
is sealed securely in the hand
of the Maker of creation.
It took an all-wise Father
to hang the stars in space,
to keep the earth
and sky
and sea
securely in their place.

God, give us eyes this Christmas
to see the Christmas star.
And give us ears to hear the song
of angels from afar.

$\mathcal{W}$ith our eyes and ears attuned
for a message from above,
let Christmas angels speak to us
of hope and faith and love.
Hope to light our pathway
when the way ahead is dark.

Hope to sing through stormy days
with the sweetness of a lark.
Faith to trust in things unseen
and know beyond all seeing
that in the Father's love
we live and have our being.
Love to break down barriers
of color, race, and creed,
Love to see and understand
and help all those in need.

If there had never been a Christmas
or the holy Christ Child's birth,
or the angels singing in the sky
of promised peace on earth.
What would the world be like today
with no eternal goal?

$\mathcal{J}$ust what would give us courage
to push on when hope is dead?
Except the Christmas message
and the words our Father said:
In love I send my only Son
to live and die for you.
And through the resurrection
you will gain a new life too.

Our father up in heaven
long, long years ago
looked down in his great mercy
upon the earth below.
And saw that folks were lonely
and lost in deep despair.
And so he said, I'll send my son
to walk among them there.

$\mathcal{S}$o they can
hear him speaking.
And feel his nearness too.
And see the many miracles
that faith alone can do.
For if man really sees him
and can touch his healing hand
I know it will be easier to believe
and understand.

$\mathcal{A}$nd so
the holy Christ Child
came down to live on earth.
That is why we celebrate
his holy, wondrous birth.
And that is why at Christmas
the world becomes aware
that heaven may seem far away
but God is everywhere.

Christmas to me is a gift from above,
a gift of salvation
born of God's love
Far beyond
what my mind comprehends.
My eternal future
completely depends
on that first Christmas
night centuries ago
when God sent his son to the earth below.
For if the Christ Child
had not been born
there would be no rejoicing
on Easter morn.
Only because Christ was born
and died
and hung on a cross
to be crucified
can worldly sinners
like you and me
be fit to live
in eternity.

So Christmas is more than
getting and giving,
it's the why and the wherefore
of infinite living.
It's the positive proof
for doubting God never.
In his kingdom
life is forever.
And that is the reason
that on Christmas Day
I can only kneel down
and prayerfully say,
"Thank you, God,
for sending your son
so when my work on earth is done
I can look at last
on your holy face,
knowing you saved me
alone
by
your
grace!"

Long, long ago
in a land far away
came the dawn
of the first Christmas day.
Each year we see
the promise reborn
God gave the world
on that first Christmas morn.
For the silent stars
in timeless skies,
the wonderment
in children's eyes,
the songs the carolers sing,
the tidings of joy
the Christmas bells ring,
remind us again
of that still, silent night
when the heavens shone
with a wondrous light,
the angels sang
of peace on earth
and told men
of the Savior's birth.

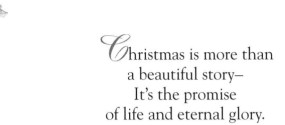

Christmas is more than
a beautiful story–
It's the promise
of life and eternal glory.

*A*ll over the world
at this season
expectant hands reach to receive gifts
that are lavishly fashioned,
the finest that man can conceive.
Purchased and given at Christmas
are luxuries we long to possess,
given as favors and tokens
to try in some way
to express that strange,
indefinable feeling
which is part of this glad time of year
when streets are crowded with shoppers
and the air resounds with good cheer.
But back of each tinsel-tied package
exchanged at this gift-giving season,
unrecognized often by many,
lies a deeper
more meaningful reason.
Born in a manger at Christmas
as a Son from the Father above,
an infant whose name is Jesus
brought mankind
the gift of God's love.

The gifts that we give have no purpose
unless God is part of the giving
and unless we make Christmas a pattern
to be followed in everyday living.

$\mathcal{A}$ star in the sky,
an angel's voice
telling the world:
Rejoice! Rejoice!
Shepherds
tending their flocks by night,
falling in awe
at this wondrous sight.
Wise men
traveling across the lands
to place their gifts
in the Christ Child's hands.
No room at the inn,
so a manger bed
cradled in radiance
the holy Babe's head.